101 USES FOR A

Bridesmaid Dress

101 USES FOR A

Bridesmaid Dress

CINDY WALKER

ILLUSTRATIONS BY

DONNA MEHALKO

William Morrow and Company, Inc. New York

It is the policy of William Morrow and Company, Inc., and its imprints and
affiliates, recognizing the importance of preserving what has been written, to print
the books we publish on acid-free paper, and we exert our best efforts to that end.

Library of Congress Cataloging-in-Publication Data
Walker, Cindy.
101 uses for a bridesmaid dress / Cindy Walker ; illustrations by Donna Mehalko.
p.   cm.
ISBN 0-688-16608-3
1. Wedding costume—Humor. 2. Clothing and dress—Remaking—Humor.
3. American wit and humor, Pictorial. I. Title. II. Title: One hundred one uses for
a bridesmaid dress III. Title: One hundred and one uses for a bridesmaid dress
TT560.W35   1999
818'.5402—dc21   98-27955
                                                                                CIP

Printed in the United States of America
First Edition
1 2 3 4 5 6 7 8 9 10
BOOK DESIGN BY CHRIS WELCH
www.williammorrow.com

To bridesmaid dresses the world over—
come out of your closets!

Foreword

We've all got bridesmaid horror stories: The dress with ruffles that added ten pounds, the $300 silk sheath in hot pink, the plunging back (perfect for winter months and pale, less-than-perfect skin), and everyone's favorite, the southern belle theme. While most of the dresses wind up hanging in the far reaches of crowded closets or bunched in old suitcases, I heard about one woman who actually dug a hole in her backyard and buried her burnt orange number. Another, who endured pink polyester during the summer, cut her dress into squares and used them to polish her car. We relate the tales with glee: Being a part of the inner circle at a close friend's wedding can be fun, but as part of postwedding etiquette we must mock the dresses.

Someplace between laughing at them and conducting burials come the ideas in this book. Ridiculous and not very practical, these suggestions are an antidote for situations like Cathy's, the woman who was made to wear the above-mentioned orange dress during a bridesmaid's worst nightmare: the Christmas wedding of a distant friend, featuring *nine* attendants in various hues of the rainbow and dresses with three ruffles across the bottom of each. To make matters worse, she was the only one not tanned from the California sun.

It's clear why Cathy had to put this dress five feet under. Still, you can get pretty silly trying to imagine just what else she might have done with it. For the last few months, in fact, it's all I've thought about. On the backs of envelopes, on napkins, in the margins of magazines, I've been collecting ideas. "Don't bury those dresses!" I cried out in encouragement to myself, muttering, "Martha Stewart, eat your heart out," as the list grew longer and longer, wackier and wilder. I felt certain that Martha would approve of the yellow silk bedroom slippers and lime-green cocktail napkins. *101 Uses* was on its way.

I hope it brings you as much pleasure as every bride feels when she's surrounded by her friends in pink tulle. I couldn't help but giggle when I came across an old bridesmaid dress in my closet recently and, with this book in mind, got out the scissors. The top of the dress became a festive halter, and the bottom . . . a pretty blanket for my stallion, Handsome. I'll wear the halter just for laughs as he and I ride the hills of my family's Virginia farm. After all, I've got plenty more to play with.

1 Use it as a matador's cape.

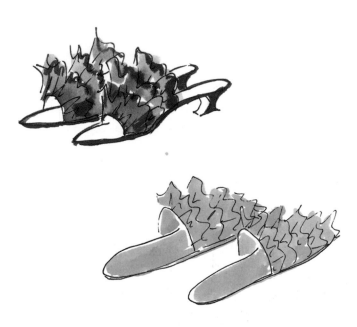

2 Make darling bedroom slippers.

3 Make uniforms for the girls' field hockey team. (Cut 'em short to make skorts.)

4 You can never have too many hair scrunchies.

5 How about a taffeta hammock?

6 The athlete in your life would love a custom jockstrap.

7 And if that's too racy . . . how about a pair of fabulous boxer shorts?

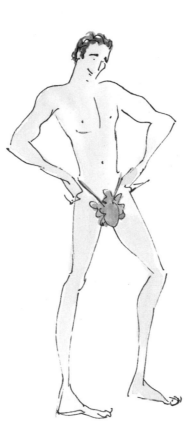

8 It makes a nifty sail.

9 Create a hang glider.

10 Jazz up your tissue boxes.

11 Or design unique cocktail napkins.

1 2 Be the hit at the Fourth of July
barbecue in your chef's toque.

1 3 If you're bored, wear it to your little
sister's prom.

14 Make your vacuum cleaner extra stylish.

15 Stuff it full of newspaper, prop it in the back of your car, and drive in the carpool lane. (You deserve it!)

1 6 A matching beach umbrella and hat
will turn heads on any beach.

17 Wear it to the opening of the new mall in town.

18 Make a ruffled skirt
for the bathroom sink.

19 Or precious little earmuffs.

20 Make spectacular baby clothes for the
couple's first child.

 21 Fashion a stylish sleeping mask for your next long flight.

22 Give the dress another chance—wear it at your IRS audit. Maybe they'll take pity on you.

23 Or on a blind date (because you were told he had such a good *personality*).

24 They make excellent waders for fly-fishing.

25 Cut yards and yards of ribbon for all your wrapping needs.

26 Make the perfect lamp shade for that romantic evening.

27 Whip up lovely silk flowers to brighten every room.

28 Dust rags—just cut into neat squares!

29 Fill it with sand and make
a punching bag.

30 Go boxing in satin workout shorts,
designed with the lightweight in mind.

31 Make handbags for all your friends.

32 Wear it to a costume ball.

33 Tie it behind your favorite kid for an instant superhero cape.

34 Create gorgeous curtains.

35 Fill it with air for an inflatable raft.

36 It makes a ritzy pool cover.

37 Use it as an awning for a lingerie store, then make some amazing underwear.

38 Make a cool raincoat (to wear over those fuchsia panties).

39 These golf club covers will stand out on the course.

40 Go even further with a set of golf pants and a cap.

41 Staying with that theme, make a beautiful sunshade for the golf cart.

42 Baby-blue silk makes the nicest little shoe bags.

43 Line your old jackets with
the fabric, too.

44 Create a line of Barbie Vegas Wear
for your young cousins.

45 Your Persian cat will appreciate her deluxe sleeping divan.

46 Have a piñata party.

47 Trim your ankle socks with ruffles.

48 Make sun visors. (Wear these and the socks to your next tennis game.)

49 Liven up your bathroom with a new
shower curtain.

50 And while you're at it, make a shower cap.

51 Jump out your frustrations with a new trampoline.

52 Keep your tea warm with a custom cozy.

53 Make booties for Fido—protect his paws from the elements.

54 Save your work clothes: Wear it to change the oil in your car.

55 A chiffon dress can make a stylish beekeeper outfit.

56 Similarly, use the light fabric for unique computer screen covers.

57 Design the tent at a dog show with your favorite frilly gown.

58 Sew a duvet for your bed.

59 And—why not?—a dust ruffle and sham to complete the look.

60 Wear your dress to guest-host
Wheel of Fortune.

61 After the show, keep it on for tea with
the Queen Mother.

⑥ ② You'll be the only one in town with these pot holders.

63 Get together with the other bridesmaids and start a quilting bee.

64 Make nifty pin cushions.

65 Earn some extra money as a psychic—you've got the perfect outfit.

66 It's just right for tea in Savannah.

67 Your lover will adore you if you wear it to dinner with his family.

68 Bake them delicacies with your newly made (satin or silk) pastry tube.

69 Then make a cheerful ice bag out of the leftover fabric—for the next morning.

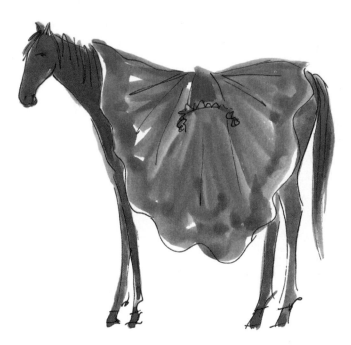

70 Depending on the size, it's an easy
pony cover or light throw for your
retired racehorse.

7 1 For the race, make new silks
for the jockeys.

72 Some simple stuffing, and you've got a vicious scarecrow.

73 Or fashion a fanciful butterfly net for those days in the park.

7 4 Give it to your kid brother
to use as a tepee.

75 A soft and sweet seat cushion will brighten every dining room table.

76 Make decorative lunch bags for the neighborhood kids.

77 Make gardening overalls: You'll look good even when you're mulching your flowers.

78 Cut it up into frost covers for your rose bushes.

79 Garnish the drumsticks on your Thanksgiving turkey.

80 Wear it to your great-uncle's birthday at the retirement home.

81 It makes divine slipcovers for your old sofa.

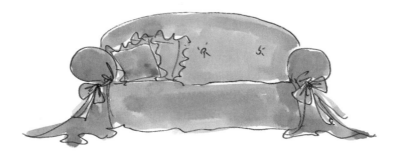

82 Be the envy of the slopes in a new
ski-bunny suit.

83 With a slight alteration, make a
jogging suit for Grandma.

84 Wear it out for New Year's Eve.

85 Create a precious cover for your diary.

86 Make turbans for those bad-hair days.

87 Design ties: Father's Day gifts for
years to come.

88 Make some nets for the high school's
basketball hoops.

89 Stitch up a radical surfboard cover.

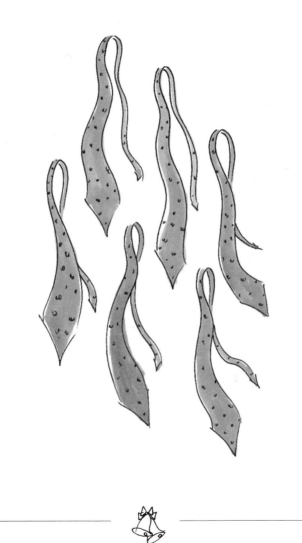

90 Throw a "Tara Revisited" party.

91 Wear it to a romance novelist convention (you can always dress it up with jewelry).

92 Make a lovely baby carriage
for the new mother.

93 Wear it to the "It's a Small World"
parade at Disney World.

94 Show up for jury duty in it—you'll be back in your office in ten minutes!

95 Cut out the middle and use it for belly dancing.

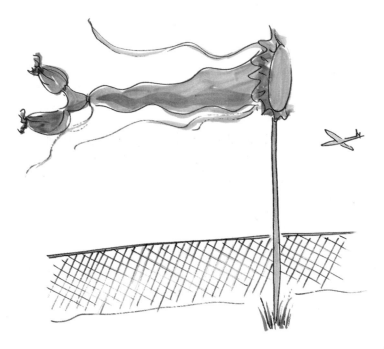

96 Provide a wind sock for
the local airport.

$\mathcal{9}\mathcal{7}$ Line the coffin of your recently departed hamster.

$\mathcal{9}\mathcal{8}$ Wear it flamenco dancing.

99 Make a toboggan for the neighborhood kids.

100 Dress up your next snowman as "Bridesmaid Frosty."

1 0 1 Blow it up for a hot air balloon—
and escape the wedding madness that seems
to descend on every bride-to-be!

Acknowledgments

This was a team effort in every way. Thanks to Elizabeth Ziemska, our agent, and Ann Treistman, our editor, and to all the brides who chose the navy blue over the sea green.

Thanks to brides with taste, Marianne Ayer Mette and Wendy Brewer Rhawn; Robin and Vic Henley, for their humorous insight; my husband, Mark; my parents, Dr. and Mrs. McBrayer; and my little sister, Christy, who holds the record for the number of times one can be a bridesmaid.
—C.W.

Thanks to my husband, John Colapinto. And to my parents, John and Helen Mehalko, for their encouragement.
—D.M.